# THE 6-FIGURE RESUME

## HOW TO WRITE EXECUTIVE RESUMES THAT GENERATE 6-FIGURE INTERVIEWS

### LISA RANGEL

# CONTENTS

*Introduction*     v

1. 12 Executive Resume Myths—Busted     1
2. Mindset, Strategy & Career Planning     5
3. How to Optimize Your Executive Resume with Keywords     13
4. The 4 Keys to Writing Your Executive Resume     21
5. How to Make Your Work Experience Shine     27
6. Education & Credentials     39
7. How to Write a Branded Summary Recruiters Can't Ignore     41
8. Layout & Design Components     47
9. The Easy Way to Format Your Resume for ATS     55
10. How to Choose the Right Resume Writing Professional for You     61

    Next Steps     65

*Appendix A*     69
*Appendix B*     75
*About the Author*     81
*Also by Lisa Rangel*     83

COPYRIGHT © 2022 Chameleon Resumes LLC

This document is intended for private, individual use only by the individual purchasing the document. Transmission, distribution, duplication or public use by any means (electronic, mechanical, recording, photocopying or otherwise) is prohibited without express written consent from Chameleon Resumes.

ISBN: 978-0-9853116-9-8

DISCLAIMER: While the author has used her best efforts in preparing and producing this ebook, she makes no guarantees, representations or warranties with the respect to the accuracy or completeness of the contents of this book and specifically disclaim any implied warranties for sale for fitness for a particular purpose. No warranty may be created or extended through affiliate or marketing partnerships in print or online sales and marketing materials. The advice and strategies contained herein are the opinions and based off client experiences of the author and may not be suitable for your situation. You should consult with a proper professional where appropriate. The author shall not be liable for any loss of profit, income or commercial damages, including but not limited to special, incidental, consequential or any other damage.

# INTRODUCTION
## A RESUME? IN THE INTERNET AGE?

Yes: even in the age of LinkedIn and digital recruitment, a top-flight executive resume is still the core document to present your experience, skills, education and achievements—and to showcase your talents.

This crucial marketing document represents you when your reputation doesn't precede you—and allows potential employers to see, at a glance, what makes you stand out from your competition.

In any economy, employers often get hundreds of resumes for each available position. An interview-generating resume is a results-driven tool that ensures your qualifications stand out from the competition. Not only does it show your skills and experience in the best possible light, it's written and formatted to cut through the screening tools employers use to discard most applicants.

The 4 Characteristics of an Interview-Generating Resume:

## 1. COMMUNICATES CONCISELY

An interview-generating resume is formatted to clearly present your strongest points in the top half of the resume, so the employer doesn't have to scroll to find them. They'll only need to scroll for specific details and additional information.

## 2. USES RESULTS-DRIVEN FORMATTING AND LANGUAGE

An interview-generating resume is organized into sections that give employers the information they want and need right away.

## 3. DESIGNED FOR IMMEDIATE IMPACT

In the waste-paper basket of traditional, dated-looking resumes, an interview-generating resume uses a crisp, professional design for strong visual appeal.

## 4. SUCCESSFULLY STANDS ALONE

Even if separated from its cover letter, an interview-generating resume still conveys to the employer exactly which position the job seeker is pursuing.

**4 Reasons Every Job Seeker Needs An Interview-Generating Resume:**

Writing your interview-generating resume in this format accomplishes four important tasks:

1. Ensures the reader knows *exactly* your area of strength or specialty.
2. Loads the document with relevant keyword phrases

in natural language to improve ATS (applicant tracking system) performance.
3. Conforms to how readers scan documents for information. People rarely take the time to read entire documents. This format keeps the reader engaged to scroll and read more.
4. Reinforces topical items of your expertise listed in the bullet section to the reader, well before they read the entire resume.

In short: a well-crafted branded resume jumps to the top of the virtual pile when you're doing a proactive job search.

So let me ask you this. What if a recruiter called today to share a great job with you? Would you be able to send a high-quality, impossible-to-ignore resume in a timely manner to reinforce your enthusiasm with quick action? Or would you need a couple of weeks to get it together?

If you were unfortunate enough to lose your job today, would your resume be ready to launch a job search fast? If not, would you be in the right frame of mind, after such a shock, to create a resume that highlights your talent?

If a promotion opened up today, would you be able to send your resume ASAP and give yourself the best possible chance of success? Or would you risk losing the opportunity with a slow response?

If you're not ready for these scenarios, you'll want to update your resume with your recent wins—and you'll want to do it now, while you still have access to your achievement data at work and when you're not under pressure to produce a resume. It is important to have a resume ready even when you are not actively looking, as demonstrated by these above scenarios.

Trust me: writing your executive resume when you are under mental stress from job loss combined with an urgency to get it done immediately to launch a search, isn't a pleasant experience—and you'll struggle to create a resume that shows you in the best possible light. The worst thing you can do is wait until you need your resume.

You owe it to yourself and your career to be prepared.

Which is where *The Ultimate Resume Writing Guide* comes in: to help you with this aspect of career self-care. This book's concepts and strategies create an executive resume that attracts attention and generates interviews—to keep your career moving forward.

Let's start with some common myths about executive resumes that may be holding you back.

# 1

# 12 EXECUTIVE RESUME MYTHS—BUSTED

Chances are, it's been a while since you updated your resume, so let's get you up to date. As an executive resume writer, I've seen many myths and misconceptions flying around that prevent great candidates from getting the jobs they want.

So before you put pen to paper I'll share some common misconceptions that hold people back—and prevent them from creating a highly effective interview-generating resume.

**Misconception # 1: Executive summaries are overrated—objectives are okay**

Objectives only state what *you* want. Summaries outline how your skills and experience can meet the prospective employer's needs. Simply put: at this stage, nobody really cares what you want.

## Misconception #2: No resume should be longer than 2 pages

It is important to realize, no matter how long you make the resume—one-page resumes included—there's no guarantee the reader will read the entire document. Easy-to-read, relevant, 5-10 second segments will keep your audience interested enough to keep scrolling and reading. If that means one page, so be it. If that's three or four pages, it's okay. The general rule for senior professionals and executives is: a two-page resume is perfectly acceptable.

## Misconception #3: Your executive resume needs charts and graphs to be impressive

I do put charts and graphs in executive resumes for some of my clients, but it's not the norm. Most clients can outline their achievements in well-written content to great effect. Charts and graphs are often not digested by applicant tracking systems (ATS), so should be used strategically and sparingly.

## Misconception #4: Jamming keywords into your executive resume gets through the ATS

While this may actually work to put your resume into human hands, when the recruiter reads your keyword-stuffed resume, they'll think you're more interested in gaming the system than showing why you're qualified for the job.

## Misconception #5: All companies use ATS systems

Not every company uses an ATS, but most have a resume database they use in some capacity. As a result, having your resume keyword-optimized is as essential as me having my coffee in the morning. You just would not want to see me without it. But—as I explained in the previous point—optimized is not the same as keyword-stuffing. Don't overdo it.

**Misconception #6: All executives who interview and hire staff should be able to write their own executive resume**

Would you be your own lawyer? Try to sell your own house? There are some people who can write their own resumes with the hiring expertise they possess. But for most of us, it's best to hire a professional—even if you have hiring expertise.

**Misconception #7: Every ounce of experience you have should be on your resume—impress the reader with everything you ever did**

As a general rule, I don't go back more than 15-20 years. Even if what you did 25 years ago is applicable to what you're targeting today, no company will hire you for what you did 25 years ago. I believe, in most cases, putting 20+ years of experience on your resume only dates you and does not really help your candidacy.

**Misconception #8: Stretch your dates to reduce or eliminate your employment gaps—no one will find out**

You can find out what your neighbor ate for dinner last night on the internet. You don't think today's background check technology can find out that you are fudging dates? Okay, they may not find out—but let's assume they will. Don't do it.

### Misconception #9: Put your references at the bottom of your resume

Don't put "references available upon request" at the bottom, there's no need. Put your references on a well-crafted reference sheet.

### Misconception #10: You can use the same resume for all your job applications and submissions

Review the job requirements and customize each submission showing how you meet the needs of the job description. One size does not fit all.

### Misconception #11: A great resume is the magic elixir to landing a job

A great resume on its own won't do it; but a great resume *with* an excellent job search plan, keyword-optimized LinkedIn profile, robust network, superb follow-up skills, and an amazing attitude—that's what'll land you a job. Even the most fabulous resume won't get you a job on its own.

### Misconception #12: My old resume will work just fine

Sure, the same way your shoulder-padded jacket or skinny tie from the 80s will work at the next Zoom company meeting. Go for it. Let me know how that works for you.

Now we've got those myths out of the way, let's get started—beginning with the most important part of all: your mindset.

# 2

# MINDSET, STRATEGY & CAREER PLANNING

How do you see your executive resume? Is it a passive document you need only when you aren't working? Or do you think of it as a marketing document that can help you strategically advance your career?

Most people mistakenly believe they need a resume only when they aren't working. This is not true—and you may be surprised to learn you are actually doing yourself a disservice waiting until you are unemployed to create your resume.

As I mentioned in the introduction, writing your resume in the immediate aftermath of the devastating blow of losing your job is the worst feeling. I often see the dread and desperation in passive job seekers; those who lost their job, and now need to write a resume fast.

It looks like this:

- They feel pressured to do their resume as quickly as possible so they can start looking for a job immediately.
- They have a "kicked in the gut" feeling that hijacks

their confidence at the exact time they need to toot their own horn. It's tough!
- They can't recall specific achievements because they no longer have access to their performance data. The company cut them off from that essential information when they were terminated.

Waiting until you desperately need a resume causes all sorts of problems, and creates added stress at at time when you really don't need it.

Think of it this way. When you manage your area or department at work, you need contingency plans and strengths/weaknesses/opportunities/threats (SWOT) analyses, so you can always be ready for the opportunities and challenges that come your way.

You do this for your company because you want to do the best you can for the people you work with.

Why wouldn't you do the same for your career, which for many people is the biggest income generator or "asset" they have?

Refreshing your resume regularly not only helps you document your achievements and milestones when the accomplishment is fresh in your mind, it helps you gauge what will move you to the next step in a proactive manner.

It's a great way to manage your own self-development.

Before you start, though, let's make sure your head is in the right place and avoid some common mindset killers—so you can craft a resume that does you credit.

## Avoid These 6 Real Resume-Writing Mindset Killers

Everyone knows the job search can be stressful and filled with hopeful ups and defeating downs. The whole thing is a bit of a rollercoaster and it's not uncommon for candidates to feel too overwhelmed to do what they need to do.

You get excited about new leads and, sometimes in the same day, suffer disappointments on your hunt for that perfect job. This is normal.

Remember that: highs and lows are normal. If you don't accept this as part of your job search, you could become your own worst enemy. You may start taking rejections personally.

Without even knowing it, you could be throwing up resistance that will kill your job hunt success and prevent you from putting your best resume out there. This resistance takes the form of physical mistakes and emotional baggage, and it hampers your ability to land that great new job.

Job hunters at all levels find themselves throwing up emotional roadblocks that will stop you in your tracks and prevent you ever setting foot in the door of the kinds of companies you want to work for.

There are many common mistakes job seekers make when looking for that next big job. Here are the six I see most often among candidates:

## 1. One-Size-Fits-All Resume and Cover Letter

One of the biggest mistakes you can make is sending the same cover letter and resume to many different companies. If you're truly interested in a position, do your homework and tailor both your resume and cover letter specifically for that position.

Which brings me to…

## 2. Research Fails

Often, candidates believe they're well-prepared for their application (and hopefully interview) by researching all they can find about the company—but they don't research the company's needs and history. They then fail to align their strengths to what the company needs.

This can cause a candidate to send off a resume that isn't tailored to specific companies, and so misses the mark. With detailed research and careful tailoring, you can craft a resume that your ideal employer will find difficult to ignore.

## 3. Talking Down Accomplishments

Many of us are taught as children not to brag and not to push ourselves forward. So I often see candidates busting a gut to appear humble—and talking down their own accomplishments. This can make it seem like they really didn't do anything of note in their past employment.

Resist the urge to be humble.

Be proud of your accomplishments. Pride is not the same as arrogance. Talk about your achievements so recruiters can see what you have to offer. Who do you think they'll offer interviews to: those who hide their best work, or those whose successes shine out?

## 4. Going It Alone

Job seekers often feel they must pursue their next job like a lonely hunter in the night. The truth is, you can get a lot of valuable information from others in your position. Talk to people who can help you.

Seek advice from recruiters, colleagues in similar positions, and job search experts—but don't rely on them as your only source of new opportunities.

## 5. Begrudging Attitude

No-one likes searching for a new job. But your attitude to your job search is crucial. Approaching it with a bad attitude only results in a poor quality resume.

Be excited about your new opportunity and enjoy the hunt

as you broaden your horizons. You may even learn a thing or two along the way.

## 6. Negative Head Trash

The biggest emotional and mental drain at the root of a stalled job search is assuming all setbacks are unique to you and happen only because you're not a desirable candidate.

It's important to realize *all* job seekers have positive and negative experiences while they search, and this is normal. Setbacks do not mean you suck. A negative experience simply means that particular employer and job opportunity was not the right one for you.

Remember, when you're crafting your resume, look at your actions objectively.

Look deep inside yourself and ask why you're having a hard time. Ask why you're not finding the type of job you want. You may discover it isn't because you simply can't find something, but that you've become your own worst enemy and you're creating unnecessary resistance in your job search.

Don't be too hard on yourself. We all indulge in negative self-talk sometimes. Just pick yourself up, recognize what you're doing, and correct it.

One of the best ways to get into the right mindset and pull yourself out of a funk is to take strategic, positive action.

So read on...

## 4 Strategic Exercises to Do Before Writing Your Resume

Each of the following exercises will help you develop a target role(s) on which to focus your resume content. Having an endgame in mind will make your executive resume more effective.

Put another way, positioning your resume to the target

audience will increase your success and maximize your compensation.

1. **Think about where you want to go next.** Look at the roles you could play in other companies both within your industry and outside your area of expertise. Evaluate transferable skills you may have and use this opportunity to learn about what you don't know yet—and possibly discover new doors opening before you.
2. Once you understand what prospective employers want to see in their next hire, it's time to **perform a self assessment**. Evaluate what you truly want to do next. Senior professionals and executives have often amassed significant achievements in many areas. They realize they're good at a lot of things—but now know they never want to do some of those activities again. And that's okay. It's time to focus on what you really want to do and highlight the talents that support your goal—and downplay the talents you don't want to use again. Brainstorm your proudest successes—the things you want to continue doing—as a foundation for your executive resume achievements. This ensures your resume reflects what you want to do in your next senior-level position.
3. **Gather examples of job descriptions or roles** you want to seek in your next career move. These may be internal promotions or external opportunities. Or why not step into the future and design your dream job to propose to your current employer or a new prospective employer?
4. **Make a list of companies you may want to work for**. Research the organizations before you write your resume so you know the areas of

opportunity and challenge your target companies face. This allows you to tailor your achievements, positioning yourself as the best person to capitalize on these opportunities and remedy the challenges the target companies experience.

By now you should feel much better prepared to write your powerful, interview-generating resume.

Move onto chapter 3 and we'll walk through how to optimize your resume with keywords.

# 3

# HOW TO OPTIMIZE YOUR EXECUTIVE RESUME WITH KEYWORDS

Your executive resume must be "search engine optimization (SEO) friendly" if you want it be found by recruiters looking for candidates like you. More specifically, this means that it has to be rich in keywords that are relevant to the position you are applying to, in order to get past the online screening process and the human reading or scanning your resume.

There is a fine line, however, between having the right number of keywords to get you through to the next level, and matching the job description so closely that the system will think you are a spammer.

This latter mistake is known as "keyword stuffing" and it won't do you any favors. In this chapter, we'll make sure you avoid looking like a spammer, and give your resume the best possible chance to float to the top of the pile.

It's a good idea to do your keyword research before you start writing your resume. It's more efficient, you'll need to do less editing, and your resume will sound more natural.

## How to Find and Incorporate Keywords Into Your Executive Resume

Here are seven ways to find keywords so you can optimize your executive resume, and ensure your resume gets passed on to recruiters.

### 1. Use the Occupational Outlook Handbook (Bureau of Labor Statistics)

The Occupational Outlook Handbook, found on the Bureau of Labor Statistics website, can be a wealth of information for executive career advancement and career changes.

Choose your target occupation (for example, Top Executive) and you will find relevant keyword clues on: What Top Executives Do, Work Environment, and How to Become a Top Executive. These profiles tend to be more specific for scientific, engineering, healthcare, and technology positions.

Yet managers, sales professionals, and creative positions are fully represented, as well.

### 2. Learn How to Use AutoCoder

AutoCoder is an effective tool from O*NET OnLine developed specifically to assign SOC 2018, O*NET 2019, and OES 2020 codes to jobs and resumes. It's a valuable tool for recruiters and job hunters.

Here's where you can get your edge: input the job title and job description for any position, and AutoCoder puts out a standard set of position matches and keywords for that role. This information helps you identify the critical keywords for that position—the same keywords that the online application system searches for.

Which means, if you include those keywords in your

resume, your resume will pop up in online application searches —leaving nothing to chance.

For example, if you were interested in landing a director of business development position, you'd run a specific job posting through the system with the title.

AutoCoder spits out a list of keywords including "sales director" and "director of marketing" as potential job titles along with information about how often certain words come up in the job description.

The frequency and score of certain phrases shows you what you need to include in your executive resume.

In the example above, you should include "sales manager," "manager," "development manager," and "business development" on your resume, weighted in value according to the frequency and score.

## 3. Target keywords through visuals

When you have a job description, you have the information you need to understand what's important to the hiring manager. Unfortunately, in text versions, it's difficult to figure out the priority of different values or the emphasis on various actions.

That's where online word cloud tools come into play. Sites like WordArt and TagCrowd allow you to enter the text of the job description, and then give you a visual representation of emphasis on the critical components.

As well as visualizing the job description, you should also get a visual for your current resume, cover letter, and any other job search materials to cross-reference keyword needs.

Once you're in the interview phase or ready to target a specific company, you can also enter the company mission statement or "about" information to get a better understanding of what they value, company-wide.

## 4. Meet the company's keywords halfway

Your resume's keywords should not only match the necessary skills for the role. They need to represent the company's overall culture and environment too. Companies are looking for employees that "complete them," just like that famous Jerry Maguire line.

Your resume should contain culture-specific references, ideals and values that are important to company culture. If you're seeking an innovative culture, then your resume should include examples of innovation and that word should be present. If you want to work at a Fortune 500 company, your resume should have that phrase in it, and so on.

Show the target companies that you possess the softer skills they seek, not only the tactical delivery of the position. Using keywords is an easy way to reinforce your overall culture fit.

## 5. Use effective language

There are few things that will confuse an online application more quickly than using the "wrong language." Many resumes do not make it through the initial screen because they contain acronyms or titles that are not widely known.

People outside your current organization may not understand the acronyms you use, so spell each of them out unless you're sure it's a widely accepted industry term. For example, an accepted and well-known acronym is GAAP, for accounting and financial positions.

Use the proper name, the universal term, *and* the acronym so all of your audiences will understand and your resume will have multiple chances to make it through the ATS system.

Job titles are often not standardized across industries or companies, so it is critical to include the right descriptive information when referring to current or previous jobs. When you use your company-specific titles only, you may end up with something like this: "Vice President."

For a human recruiter or online system, it is very unclear what your actual duties were as a "vice president." You're missing a functional or departmental descriptor, something like: Vice President, Internet Marketing. Be sure to include these details in your executive resume.

## 6. Use SEO (Search Engine Optimization) techniques to optimize your resume

An SEO approach will help you to enhance your resume with keywords. This increases your odds of getting through the initial "robot" review of your resume, and help put your resume in the hands of the hiring manager.

Not only will this approach help the right people see your resume, it will also increase your subject matter credibility, instantly.

Learn optimization techniques from websites such as SearchEngineJournal.com, SocialMediaExaminer.com, and SearchEngineLand.com. They'll show you how to discover keyword phrases so you can use the best processes and tactics to construct your resume.

Once you learn these techniques, hop over to Google AdWords Keyword Planner, open a free account, and start to home in on the right keywords for your target position, based on the information you've discovered so far from the previous five tactics.

## 7. Three ways to use LinkedIn to obtain suggested keywords and phrases

Firstly, did you know you can use LinkedIn Skills to determine previously used keywords that may be most common for what you do?

Secondly, you can also try searching specific terms using the LinkedIn search bar. The predetermined keywords that show up in the drop-down menu can be a good indicator of what most people who do your job search for most often.

Finally, look for profiles similar to yours, doing similar or identical jobs. Review what seem to be relevant keywords in their profile and consider incorporating them uniquely and naturally in your resume.

Using these tools to identify the right keywords allows you to use them effectively in your resume—so you can optimize your resume expertly.

The best plan is to send your resume directly to a human—but failing that, you need to make sure that your resume can beat the technology. After all, your resume may sit online until the right match comes along.

The overall goal here is for a technical search to find your resume fast.

## Core Competencies

The Core Competencies section of your resume is one of the places you can really leverage the keyword optimization strategies listed above to make your resume highly tailored for the job you're applying for.

Use keywords from target job descriptions that reflect your relevant accomplishments. Use topical nouns instead of verbs to highlight your skills and increase recognition from the applicant tracking system software.

- ✓ Strategic Business Planning and Execution
- ✓ Integrated Front, Middle and Back Office Operations
- ✓ Complex Change Management
- ✓ High Productivity with Collaborative Approachability
- ✓ Global Expertise in Europe, Asia and Africa
- ✓ Fiscal Accountability and P&L Management
- ✓ Mergers, Acquisitions and System Integration
- ✓ Cross-Cultural Talent Training and Development
- ✓ Large Client Relationship Management
- ✓ Risk Management and Performance Metrics

This is a great place to grab an executive recruiter's

attention by highlighting your technology expertise. In today's post-pandemic world where companies are making full use of online programs and computer software to help them streamline their businesses, it's imperative to show you're up-to-date on all the changes.

You can use your technology expertise to beef up your resume's Skills Section. For instance, if you're heavily involved with your current company's sales department, you'll want to note that you're familiar with the software they use (like Salesforce or other popular client relationship managers).

If you work in an extremely technical field, such as healthcare, you'll want to use the long-form version as well as the abbreviated version of any technology or software. The reason being that when recruiters look for you on LinkedIn or in their own applicant tracking system sometimes they won't think to search for both forms.

Finally, if applicable, this would be the perfect place to mention any technical certifications you hold. For instance, CIO's should be familiar with all the different networking and IT certifications out there. This often requires that your certifications be up-to-date.

# 4

## THE 4 KEYS TO WRITING YOUR EXECUTIVE RESUME

Amazing that the "writing your resume" section of the ultimate resume book is the fourth chapter, eh? There is a lot of pre-work to do before you start writing—but that pre-work will make your resume a far more effective document. So kudos to you for engaging chapters 1 through 4.

When you've completed your market research, decided on your target companies and roles, completed your self-assessment of what you want to do next, and done keyword research coupled with planning your resume structure, you can now start to write the content for your resume.

Follow these guidelines and you'll stand out as the best candidate to hire, whether you're in the public, private or non-profit sector.

There are four key pieces of information you'll need to give your target audience throughout the multiple sections of your resume:

## Who?

Rather than beginning your resume with an objective, use a title—as shown in this Chief Operations Officer resume sample below. You may want to include a brief elevator-style pitch below the title, succinctly outlining why a company should hire you. This should serve as a compelling positioning statement, setting the stage for the rest of your resume.

Consider including the most relevant achievements and qualifications, such as degrees earned or any professional certifications. Space on your resume is valuable, so ensure any qualifications you choose to include in the Summary and Employment Sections connect the dots between your target roles and current competencies.

---

**GLOBAL HEAD OF OPERATIONS**

*Cross-Geographical & Cultural Team Integration | Strategic Business Unit Development & Execution*

Operations Leader with an indelible reputation for delivering inventive business strategies and client-focused solutions that improve margins. Recognized for transforming multimillion dollar global operations profitably and efficiently.

Broad experience building profitable start-up divisions, growth business lines, deal transactions and streamlined operations. Mobilizes top-tier talent to create high performing cultures that consistently achieve in volatile markets.

---

## What?

It's helpful for someone viewing your resume for the first time to see what your topical expertise is. When addressing relevant topical items in your resume under the Core Competency Section, as shown in this executive resume sample, you fulfill the keyword optimization required by humans reading your document *and* resume databases digesting your document.

Provide an overview of your areas of expertise (finance, operations, sales, marketing), which industries you've been exposed to (consulting, manufacturing, food and beverage, consumer goods), and your levels of responsibility.

This will provide context for your achievements and core strengths.

- ✓ Strategic Business Planning and Execution
- ✓ Integrated Front, Middle and Back Office Operations
- ✓ Complex Change Management
- ✓ High Productivity with Collaborative Approachability
- ✓ Global Expertise in Europe, Asia and Africa
- ✓ Fiscal Accountability and P&L Management
- ✓ Mergers, Acquisitions and System Integration
- ✓ Cross-Cultural Talent Training and Development
- ✓ Large Client Relationship Management
- ✓ Risk Management and Performance Metrics

## Where?

Following on from the last point, explain (briefly) what each organization did, and put it into perspective. Was it publicly or privately held? Regional, national, or global? What markets and regions did you work within?

It may be helpful to describe the size of the workforce or the company's annual revenue. Don't assume everyone is familiar with individual companies or even the industries. The example below shows how you can effectively define size and scope when describing current and previous employers.

---

Executive Leadership Roles Held at Chase Beacon Financial, Chatham Investment and Stanford Partners

**STANFORD PARTNERS, INC.** | New York, NY    November 2016 – Present
*Financial leader with $8.5B in revenue and 11,750 employees in offices across 37 countries, providing investment funds and global custody services*
**Senior Vice President, Investment Management Services & Client Services Group**
Hand-selected by Stanford Partners (SP) to direct the strategic integration of the $350M acquisition of Chatham Investment Management's (CIM) global operations and its 110-person staff. Reported to the Executive Vice President of Investment Management Services, directed four VPs supporting global client relations and managed a 33-member team.

---

## How?

Demonstrating performance is crucial, particularly at executive level. Let your accomplishments speak for themselves. Provide evidence through specific examples—what you achieved, when, and where—that will also implicitly communicate your mastery of your profession.

Sales success is easy to quantify, but other functions might not translate as easily to numbers. You may be able to point to cost savings you achieved, processes you made more efficient, productivity increases, employee relations improved, projects delivered on time and on budget, risks mitigated, or other initiatives successfully deployed.

Use active verbs that reflect your role in each. Don't waste time with generic and empty adjectives. I've included an Action Verb Guide in the appendices to help you do this.

Here are some other questions to ask yourself when building your executive resume:

- How have you been involved in setting a vision and carrying out strategy for organizations? How have you used "big picture" thinking to initiate change?
- Have you hired, fired, and built teams? What about personal development—have you mentored more junior employees?
- Have you been responsible for budgets, fundraising, high-level negotiations, or other financial matters?
- Have you been involved in any mergers or acquisitions, or other major business initiatives you can point to?
- What kinds of business relationships do you have and at what level? How do you deal with stakeholders, clients, and suppliers? Do you have a valuable network of contacts?
- What kind of experience do you have with public speaking, writing, or giving presentations? How have you represented your organization to the community and the wider public?

- **Facilitated Acquisition Negotiations:** Appointed to execute deliverables stemming from the SP/CIM negotiations and served as the intermediary during acquisition negotiations.
    - Oversaw the multi-year $27M technology integration and conversion project to migrate trading operations to an industry-leading data service platform that accommodated the acquired CIM middle market function.
    - Managed 2012 P&L $35M CIM revenue budget, a main client account for the firm.
- **Streamlined Client Services Processes:** Developed client relationships, restructured client delivery processes and improved shared service operational controls, increasing profit margins by 2.9%.
    - Authorized contractual commitments to provide services or meet deliverables.
    - Successfully managed ongoing client service reviews and recorded key performance indicator data, in collaboration with other departments, ensuring client service expectations were fulfilled consistently.
    - Collaborated with operations teams to develop and implement recommendations for service improvement.
- **Improved Global Risk Programs:** Established Key Risk Indicators to guide investment activity, resulting in a 24% decrease in loss reserves used and contributing to 86% of funds performing ahead of prior year.
- **Margin & Revenue Growth:** Increased margins by 14% and revenues by 27% with pricing and cross-selling initiatives.

Client Revenue Budget
$35 Million

Technology Integration Budget
$27 Million

Acquisition Size
$350 Million in Assets

## Outline Your Resume

You should now have a plan for writing the details of your executive resume. The major sections are:

- Title and contact details
- Executive summary with headline
- Work experience
- Skills
- Education

Although the executive summary is the first thing a recruiter will see on your resume, it should be the last thing you write—it'll be much easier to do once you've written the rest of your resume.

Starting with your work experience, in the next chapter.

# 5

# HOW TO MAKE YOUR WORK EXPERIENCE SHINE

Here's a pill that may be tough to swallow: most people have lackluster resumes. They tend to write extremely generic resumes that only showcase basic job duties. As a result, recruiters think they're dealing with someone who can only do the basics.

Here's the tragedy: most people have done great work that has made a real difference in the companies they've worked in —but don't know how to showcase it. This can be fixed!

Achievement-based resumes help you stand out from the crowd because they give concrete examples of what you can do on the job.

Achievements are those wins that made a lasting impact on the company or the client. In this chapter, I'll walk you through how to write an achievement-based executive resume.

## How to Write an Achievement-Based Executive Resume

Here's an example of a typical work experience summary, before we worked on it:

## JON X. SMITH

1425 Aspen Lane
Wyckoff, NJ 10198
(201) 555-5494
jonxsmith@dartmotuh.edu

### SUMMARY

Results oriented securities industry executive with a consistent record of demonstrating leadership in complex, global businesses. Proven track record of developing business unit strategies and managing large transformational change.

- Proven leader recognized for successful track record of creating high performance cultures that attract, develop and retain diverse talent for global financial businesses
- Expert manager of large operations recognized for ability to execute
- Trusted service partner with a reputation for delivering innovative, client focused business strategies and solutions

### CAREER HISTORY

**STANFORD PARTNERS**, New York, New York
**Senior Vice President, November 2014- Present**

- Joined firm as the most senior executive of a lift-out transaction in which Chatham Investment Management outsourced its global middle and back office functions to Stanford Partners in November 2014
- Global relationship and business executive for Chatham client account, responsible for direct operational management of portfolio services business operations teams as well as global oversight of large-scale conversion and integration program to transition CIM business to Stanford Street middle-office platform. Also responsible for global client P&L, strategic account plans, cross-selling/new products, achievement of Critical Service and Key Performance indicators, and overall client satisfaction

And here's an example of an effective work experience summary pulled from an executive resume using the achievement-centric style:

## PROFESSIONAL EXPERIENCE

Executive Leadership Roles Held at Chase Beacon Financial, Chatham Investment and Stanford Partners

**STANFORD PARTNERS, INC.** | New York, NY                            **November 2016 – Present**

*Financial leader with $8.5B in revenue and 11,750 employees in offices across 37 countries, providing investment funds and global custody services.*

**Senior Vice President, Investment Management Services & Client Services Group**

Hand-selected by Stanford Partners (SP) to direct the strategic integration of the $350M acquisition of Chatham Investment Management's (CIM) global operations and its 110-person staff. Reported to the Executive Vice President of Investment Management Services, directed four VPs supporting global client relations and managed a 33-member team.

- **Facilitated Acquisition Negotiations:** Appointed to execute deliverables stemming from the SP/CIM negotiations and served as the intermediary during acquisition negotiations.
    - Oversaw the multi-year $27M technology integration and conversion project to migrate trading operations to an industry-leading data service platform that accommodated the acquired CIM middle market function.
    - Managed 2012 P&L $35M CIM revenue budget, a main client account for the firm.
- **Streamlined Client Services Processes:** Developed client relationships, restructured client delivery processes and improved shared service operational controls, increasing profit margins by 2.9%.
    - Authorized contractual commitments to provide services or meet deliverables.
    - Successfully managed ongoing client service reviews and recorded key performance indicator data, in collaboration with other departments, ensuring client service expectations were fulfilled consistently.
    - Collaborated with operations teams to develop and implement recommendations for service improvement.
- **Improved Global Risk Programs:** Established Key Risk Indicators to guide investment activity, resulting in a 24% decrease in loss reserves used and contributing to 86% of funds performing ahead of prior year.
- **Margin & Revenue Growth:** Increased margins by 14% and revenues by 27% with pricing and cross-selling initiatives.

| Client Revenue Budget |
|---|
| $35 Million |
| **Technology Integration Budget** |
| $27 Million |
| **Acquisition Size** |
| $350 Million in Assets |

### Embrace more interesting verbs

Oftentimes people fail to use specific verbs in a resume, which leads to a boring depiction of what they actually did on the job. Anyone can say "worked in accounting," but that doesn't really say anything about what your job entailed. Consider using verbs that stand out, such as "spearheaded" or "streamlined."

### Don't shy away from highlighting your accomplishments

As I mentioned in Chapter 2, many people don't give themselves enough credit because they believe they sound like they're bragging. But a resume doesn't require humility or bragging—resumes require facts. If you did something, and it's a fact, then it isn't bragging. Conveying these facts to recruiters via your resume tells them why you're the right fit for the job!

So be sure to highlight your accomplishments in your resume.

Start with any awards and recognitions you received while on the job. You can then list other achievements that perhaps you didn't get public recognition for.

During the COVID period, many executives and senior professionals have more non-measurable achievements: improving employee morale, creating flexible work schedules, and building effective remote work systems are good examples. Include what is traditionally measured *and* what has recently risen in importance and, from there, you can narrow down the best choices and write them in bullet form.

**Show them your results**

Recruiters want to see that you produce results. You can do this in several ways, by providing examples of how you saved a company money, increased revenue, or increased team productivity.

Don't expand your stories in paragraph form on the resume (save those for the interview). Instead, keep to a simple bullet point form to grab your reader's attention and pique their interest.

Give the recruiter a reason to invite you to an interview so they can learn more about what you did.

**Add numbers to those results**

Using quantitative examples (examples that include numbers) paints a clear picture for the person reading your resume.

One key question to ask yourself when trying to quantify your contributions is, "By how much?"

For instance, perhaps you increased company revenue. This is a great achievement to highlight, but you can't just leave it at that. This is when you ask yourself, "By how much?"

Remind yourself to find the numbers that prove it. You may not be able to get your hands on sales reports or other confidential information, especially without giving away the fact that you're up to something (in this case looking for work elsewhere). If this is the case and you're planning ahead, you can always start tracking your own progress a few weeks in advance.

**Highlight something you initiated voluntarily**

Recruiters always have an eye out for self-starters. After all, once you get to a certain level the last thing they want is someone who needs to be micromanaged. This is why it's a good idea to highlight projects you initiated yourself.

Did you get new business on your own? Did you volunteer to put the company 5k together? Are you mentoring other employees out of the goodness of your heart? These are all great examples of how you set out to achieve things on your own.

Writing an achievement-based resume is an effective way to highlight why you're a great fit for the job. By showcasing your successes you give the recruiter exactly what they're looking for right off the bat.

**The Secrets of Writing Achievement-Based Executive Resume Bullets**

An achievement-based executive resume focuses on the specifics of what you accomplished at your previous jobs. Ideally, this type of resume gives concrete examples of what you can do for your potential employer.

Using bullet points is a sure-fire way to stand out from the crowd and increase your chances of being called in for an interview. Use the tips below to make the most of your resume bullets.

## Focus On CAR Stories

Using well-respected interview techniques can help you focus on your achievements, and make your resume writing process a lot easier.

CAR, for instance, stands for Context, Action, Result. It's a framework for telling a short story that conveys a lot of information in a small space. The context is the problem your previous employer had. The action is the action you took to solve that problem. And the result is what you achieved. Stories are compelling, and this type of story shows you as the hero in the situation.

When writing each bullet you can call upon this technique to help you find the most important information. Obviously, you don't have room to go into the entire story on your resume, but you can use it to help you find the achievements—and as a bonus, you'll be well-prepared for any interviews in which you'll need to expand on those achievements.

Let's say you were global operations director at a previous company, which was running up against a major sales deficit. Your current model wasn't working. You thought that if you adjusted pricing and focused on some cross-selling, you might see improvements. The end result was a huge increase in company revenue.

A bullet, in this case, may read, "Increased margins by 14% and revenues by 27% with pricing and cross-selling initiatives."

## Ask key questions while writing resume bullets

For every job description bullet, ask, "How do you know you did a good job?" or "What did that good job look like?"

This helps you focus on the results you achieved at work. Ultimately, by painting a picture for yourself, you can do the same for the person reviewing your resume.

These numbers may not be so focused on revenue numbers, and that's okay. For example, if you're an HR executive you may have helped expand the company into new markets. That may read like this: "Led HR function on 2019 Asian expansion, which currently has 240 offices and 7,000 employees."

**Focus on size of company/department and scope of environments**

When it comes to resumes, numbers talk. Figures can be extremely revealing about what kind of environment you worked in and the results you achieved.

For instance, strategic planning for a $5 million startup tech firm is a different job than strategic planning for a $200 million division of a $1.7 billion consumer products firm.

So be specific with business situations when describing duties. This is when you can mention the size of budgets, number of employees, and how much a company is worth.

**4 Rarely-Discussed Strategies: How Far Back Should I Go on My Executive Resume?**

It's a good question—and, as with most tactical executive resume questions, I'm afraid the answer is "it depends".

However, when we work with executive-level clients with 15-35 years experience, we do use guidelines when making decisions about how much information to include and how far back to go.

Generally speaking, we recommend focusing on the most recent 15-20 years of work experience, but this can vary based on each individual. The nature of the work experience and the various forms it can take when compared to the target positions is the main factor in determining if we will consider using older information on a resume.

## 1. Pedigree of the Organization Pertaining to the Profession

If the executive job seeker is a CFO with a CPA credential, and the earlier CPA firm experience is with PWC back in 2000, then we'd put this into the resume. The reason for this decision is the caliber and relevancy of this experience.

The caliber of training and professional development a CFO had in their early career can be pertinent to many hiring managers. If the caliber of earlier employment is not impressive or does not communicate quality training, it may be best left off the resume.

## 2. Pioneering Status of the Company Pertaining to the Industry

A leading digital entertainment or media executive may have started their career in the advertising department, working on the Nike account in the 1990s. Working for pioneering firms in the marketing, entertainment, and digital spaces can showcase this person's reputation as a consistent trailblazer in these industries, if their work experience shows a pattern.

For this candidate, we would create a "prior work experience" section after the most recent 15 years of work experience to cite the company and role without dates.

If the job seeker has not maintained working for pioneering organizations, it may be best to leave off the early information, as it may unnecessarily date the candidate.

## 3. Proof of Desirable Traits Throughout Career

This part is essential for career changes, but anyone can benefit from this tactic if the experience is relevant. Starting out in my career, I graduated from the Cornell Hotel School and went on to work for the premium hotel chains, Four Seasons Hotels and Pebble Beach Company.

What does that have to do with recruiting, executive resume writing, and job search coaching? Directly? Not much… but I have been hired by staffing firms (in the past) and by clients (currently) who see that I have a high-caliber service background. They believe the skills I honed will be carried throughout all my pursuits—and they are correct!

This top quality and service mentality seeps into everything I do.

When job seekers have experience that demonstrates such desirable traits, and it is relevant to a career change or promotion, it's beneficial to include earlier experiences that show this pattern.

## 4. Industry or Profession Dictate Best Practice

Some industries, such as healthcare, find it more valuable if their executives have more experience than less. In these cases, we go back to college graduation, no matter how long ago they graduated.

Advertising industries, on the other hand, value the new experiences, so we focus on the most recent accomplishments in a resume.

Based on the candidate's target job prospects, we look at what will be most relevant and helpful to showcase what is valued by that industry and profession.

## How to Phrase it Right: a Guide to Challenging Situations

The most important objective when presenting any sort of anomaly in your resume is to do so without distracting the reader from your qualifications. It's crucial to present your information in such a way that it answers the question, "What did they do during that time?" without generating confusion.

When a reader is confused or distracted by side questions, they're not focused on your experience. You want the reader to evaluate your qualifications and consider you for an interview, by turning anything that could be problematic into a non-issue. Here are suggested treatments for handling some common situations.

**Gap in Your Resume**

If you have a gap in your resume over 10 years ago, minimize it by playing up your experience before and after the gap. If it is a significant gap of more than four years, consider adding a line that neutrally explains what took place during that period.

You can populate this section with volunteer activities and other community leadership roles you may have had during this time. Here are a few examples:

- Stay-at-home parent: 2013-2017
- Full time student: 2010-2014
- Personal leave: 2012-2014. Perhaps this would be caring for a sick parent or personal medical leave. All you need is a simple phrase accounting for the time.
- Professional research sabbatical: 2009-2011. If you use this, be sure to include the activities and findings to back it up.

**Promoted Multiple Times at the Same Job**

Congratulations! The key here is to have your information visually represent the promotions. The most common mistake job seekers make here is to format the information so it looks like they had lots of short jobs at separate companies—the complete opposite of what they intend to communicate!

Use the suggested format below to make it clear to the

reader that you're on a progressive upward path in your career. There are several additional examples of how to handle this situation in the Sample Resumes appendix.

BANANA REPUBLIC, New York, NY & Princeton, NJ
November 2014 – July 2019

Purchasing Manager (October 2017 to July 2019)

- Purchased, bid and maintained inventory levels of all non-merchandise items for the company's 750 stores nationwide, 4 Distribution Centers, Corporate Operations Office and the Canadian Home Office.

Assistant Manager (November 2015 to October 2017)

- Managed 24-employee staff and inventory for a $1.5 million dollar store in Central New Jersey.

Store Associate (November 2014 to November 2015)

## Company Mergers or Renames

Companies are often merged or renamed, which can create confusion when listing work experience. The solution is to name the company you work/worked for and, in parentheses, give the current name of the company or the company with which it merged. Include the year of the change.

For example:

Johnson Promotions (now Branded Images, Inc. as of 2017), Houston, TX August 2010 – January 2014

AccountPros (merged with Accountants International in 2015), NY, NY April 2012 – February 2014

## How to Handle a Layoff

Handling a layoff is more of a discussion strategy when preparing for an interview. It shouldn't really come into your resume.

In most situations, you don't include any details about how or why you leave a position on your resume, unless it's related to a business activity like a merger, acquisition, or corporate relocation. If your layoff is the result of one of these situations, you can mention the situation on your resume (as explained above) and have the reader infer that is why you are no longer there.

Here are some examples:

Nimble Storage (Acquired by Hewlett Packard Enterprise), San Jose, CA Product Engineer

Social Media Week (Acquired by Adweek in 2021), , New York, NY Client Accounting Manager

## Keep it Brief

Keep your work experience section as succinct as possible, sticking to the most recent 15-20 years—unless there's a strong reason to go further back.

Remember: most resumes look the same. The idea here is to make you stand out, so don't be afraid to showcase your achievements and highlight your successes. Use the principles of storytelling to create a compelling resume and encourage recruiters to invite you to an interview, so they can find out more.

Now it's time to move onto the next section: education.

# 6

## EDUCATION & CREDENTIALS

We're getting to the bottom of your resume now. This is where you can talk about your education, certifications, trainings, and any other relevant credentials.

You can choose to exclude dates for degrees over 15-20 years old, but some people do prefer to leave the dates in. It's a strategic decision whether to include it or not. Is your degree crucial to what you do? Does it set you apart in some way from other candidates? If so, include it.

If not, you might want to leave it out.

The key is to be consistent in what you choose to include or exclude.

When writing about your degree, include your degree name, university, major, and date of graduation for each education credential. You only need to include your GPA if you have less than five years' experience in the financial sector. For senior professionals and executives, GPAs are rarely required.

## Education

**MASTERS OF BUSINESS ADMINISTRATION** | NOTRE DAME UNIVERSITY
**BACHELOR OF SCIENCE, ELECTRICAL ENGINEERING** | UNIVERSITY OF FLORIDA

## Professional Development

**CERTIFIED FACILITIES HOSPITALITY EXECUTIVE (CFHE)** - AMERICAN HOTEL AND LODGING EDUCATIONAL INSTITUTE
**LEED GREEN ASSOCIATE** - GREEN BUSINESS CERTIFICATION INSTITUTE
**ISSP-SA PROFESSIONAL CERTIFICATION** - GREEN BUSINESS CERTIFICATION INSTITUTE

# 7

# HOW TO WRITE A BRANDED SUMMARY RECRUITERS CAN'T IGNORE

The unique strength of an Interview-Generating Executive Resume comes from its opening section—the Branded Summary. A Branded Summary encapsulates what you have done and what you can do for a prospective employer.

This highly focused section will get attention in resume databases and from recruiters who use keywords.

Now the body of your resume is completed (the Employment, Education and any other sections), you can start working on this essential piece. There are examples of how it should look on the following page and in the Sample Resumes appendix.

Here are the four steps you need to take to create this impactful resume opener.

1. Assign yourself a title that reflects the job you're seeking and the experience you have thus far.

2. Write a descriptive summary paragraph under your branded title utilizing the following structure:

- First sentence captures the value you'll bring to the employer.
- Second sentence demonstrates how you'll solve problems.
- Third sentence communicates soft skills that add value to the position for which you are applying.

3. Create a list of bulleted skills and topical items you'll place under your summary paragraph:

- Noun-based (not verb-based) bullets to reinforce your qualifications in a concise format.
- Keyword phrases for optimum recruiter searching.
- Phrases derived from your past performance evaluations or from job ads.

4. Use a border from the MS Word Borders & Shading function at the top and bottom of the section to frame your resume. Choose a design that promotes the image you want to convey.

Three items that should NOT be included in your Interview-Generating Branded Summary section:

1. Never use the title "Objective."
2. Never use first person.
3. Do not state what you're looking for, what skills you want to develop, what training you seek, or anything else you want. This section is not about what you want. It is about what value, results, experience, and concrete skills you bring to the prospective employer.

Hiring managers are increasingly pressed for time as they scan hundreds of resumes looking for the perfect candidate. A top-notch Branded Resume Summary could be the thing that convinces the recruit to read your resume—instead of tossing it into the trash with the rest of them.

You may think the interview is the most difficult part of your job search, but the truth is getting your foot in the door and getting an opportunity for an interview is often far more difficult. However, you can improve your chances just by crafting a compelling executive resume summary.

A well-crafted executive resume summary will help you get noticed and allow you to quickly put your best foot forward so hiring managers will give your resume a closer look.

## The 7 Must-Have Components of an Eye-Catching Executive Resume Summary

### 1. Format Your Summary Title Carefully

I make the target title slightly bigger than the candidate name. Some executive resume writers make the candidate name bigger so the hiring manager can always find the name and know they're on the right resume.

But at first glance, the name doesn't really matter. As a hiring manager, I wanted to know if this person was right for the job I was recruiting for. During my 13-year recruiting career, I always found a resume with a bigger title helped me make an assessment faster—if it was the right candidate. The name had nothing to do with my assessment.

So I recommend the summary title be slightly bigger than the name.

> **CHIEF FINANCIAL OFFICER**
> *Supporting growth of businesses by delivering financial advisory and insight to Executives*
>
> International Finance Executive with experience across several disciplines including FP&A, M&A integration, finance operations, and cost reduction. Builds and leads high-performance teams, aligned with objectives surrounding profitability and growth. Sought after financial advisor and valued resource to operations, critical to generating financial success. Well-rounded leadership background with expertise working directly with Executive Management. Enables business excellence by challenging status quo and leveraging innovative strategies to ensure strong financial returns for multibillion-dollar companies.
>
> ⇨ Served as Interim Chief Financial Officer for late-stage digital media start-up (DigitalRich), supporting business restructuring; partnered with business unit leaders to reduce costs by 15-20% across international offices, news division, and advertising sales team.
>
> ⇨ Demonstrated success in FP&A and Investor Relations at major organizations including VeltexTV ($57B in revenue) and QRSGlobal ($35B+ in revenue); served as trusted and valuable partner to CEOs and CFOs.

## 2. Cite a Specific Position in the Title

Hiring managers scan hundreds of resumes when they search for the right candidate. Studies show recruiters often make the decision to call you or discard your resume in seconds. So, you need to hook them quickly if you hope to have a shot.

When creating your summary, begin with something that will grab attention and encourage them to read on. This will increase your chances of making it into the call pile.

Do not start the heading with the word "SUMMARY."

And don't use a broad, all-encompassing title in the hope you'll avoid being pigeon-holed. An all-encompassing title has an unexpected detrimental effect: when you try to appeal to everyone, you end up appealing to no one.

## 3. Emphasize Your Top Selling Points

Once you have their attention, emphasize your best selling points—the ones that demonstrate why *you* are the right person for the job.

When hiring managers search, they skim resumes fast looking for the right criteria. To increase your chances, put your best foot forward right away, and show them what makes you the best candidate for the job.

## 4. Correlate Career Achievements to Job Requirements

Once you have the recruiter reading and they know your best selling points, it's time to briefly go over your career to show how your experience is relevant to their position.

This gives them an insight into your experience so they can begin to understand what you bring to the table if they decide to call you in for an interview.

## 5. Communicate Your Motivation

The simple objective statement may be out of style today, but that doesn't mean you can't briefly share your motivation, when applicable.

Each company is different, with a different culture and goals.

If your motivation doesn't fit their mold, you may not be a good fit, even if you have all the skills they're looking for. This isn't good for them or you in the long run.

Go ahead and briefly explain your goals, but don't give it too much weight compared to your selling points and career.

## 6. Be Concise

You may be tempted to go into great detail about your career and your top selling points. Remember, you have the rest of your resume to explain everything you've accomplished and show why you would be the perfect candidate for the position.

The goal with your summary is to provide just that—a summary. Resist the urge to explain everything in detail. Give them a glimpse of what you've done over the years and if it's compelling enough, they'll want to read on.

## 7. Don't Underestimate the Power of Keywords

You should never just write your resume for keywords, but don't forget about them entirely. When writing your summary, make sure it's rich in keywords so it makes it past the automatic resume scanners and actually reaches the desk of the hiring manager.

# 8

## LAYOUT & DESIGN COMPONENTS

First and foremost, your resume needs to be easy to read.

As a former search firm recruiter, I am often asked, "How long do you take to read a resume?"

Really that question is based on an incorrect assumption. Most recruiters don't truly "read" resumes. Resumes are scanned by recruiters the way most of us scan websites looking for information. Think about the last time you did a web search and started clicking through the results. We don't actually 'read' every word on a website. We visually scan them looking for specific keywords and phrases to assess if we should keep reading to click through further or if we should move on to the next search result.

That visual scanning process can take most of us 10-15 seconds. Similarly, your resume may be getting as little as 6 seconds of attention (according to The Ladders studies done in 2012 and 2018) before a recruiter or hiring manager decides to dig deeper into your resume or pass your resume by for the next candidate.

## How to Format Your Executive Resume

Start with a clean MS Word document. Use only the MS Word Borders and Shading function for simple graphic treatment to increase digestion with the ATS (Applicant Tracking Systems). Envision your resume being written concisely.

Format your executive resume using white space and a balance of prose and bullets. This format leads the eye through the document. You don't have a lot of room on the screen of a mobile phone, so your summary is to the point. Use one line to describe the company environment for each employment section to give your accomplishments context. Make sure your achievements are bulleted. Avoid big blocks of text and long bulleted lists.

Plan to test your resume on different devices to ensure it opens properly. Mobile recruiting doesn't always refer to a phone, it includes tablets too. Furthermore, an Android phone and an iPhone have different screen sizes and programs for opening documents such as PDFs.

Check for how it reads on the screen (you don't want any words being cut off) and if it even opens at all. There's nothing more embarrassing than sending your resume to someone and having them not be able to open it.

## Contact Information

The first component of your resume will be your contact information. Your name should be larger than the main font, but not the largest font. Put your name at the top of the document, whether you center, right, or left align. Place your contact information in the document body and not the header or footer. If you went to a reputable or well-networked school, use your .edu email address. Use a mobile phone number so you can accept texts. Include your LinkedIn vanity URL.

> PAT MARINA
> Marketown, MA 18702 • 555.469.5080 • patmarina@gmail.com • www.linkedin.com/in/patmarinax/
> **EVP OF MARKETING | CHIEF MARKETING OFFICER**
> Trusted leader who inspires teams to consistently exceed corporate goals humanly

## The Executive Resume Heading Title

This title section under your contact information is considered prime resume real estate. Do not use the word SUMMARY in this section. You are wasting important space.

Instead, use this area to make a heading title that reflects the position you want. Make it as easy for the executive recruiter as possible by showing them what role you are seeking/applying for by submitting your resume.

Handing in a resume for a high-level position without a title may cost you the interview, since you're failing to give the person reading your resume any idea of the role you want. Many recruiters won't take the time to figure it out.

You can fix this by using a descriptive title at the top of the resume.

For instance, use titles such as " Chief Financial Officer" or "Director of Accounting" or "Vice-President of Finance" Do not be vague with general areas, such as "Accounting." Instead, be specific and always use a title or combination of two similar titles.

The same concept can be applied to a number of positions in departments across the board. The point is to tell the reader exactly what you do in a quickly.

For example, if you typically use the generic heading title of Marketing Executive, but are applying for a Marketing Director position, update your heading to: Marketing Director. There is no guessing left for the recruiter and you will have piqued the recruiter's interest from the very beginning.

| GLOBAL HEAD OF OPERATIONS |
|---|

Chief Financial Officer • Multinational Manufacturing

| CHIEF MEDICAL OFFICER |
|---|

Important note: if you are not applying for a specific position, but are seeking general opportunities or an exploratory interview, use your broad title – in the example above Marketing Executive/Director, to be considered for various roles.

Place your contact information in the body of the MS Word document. Do not place it in a header or a footer, as the content in the sections is often not downloaded into ATS and/or not readable in email previewers.

Include your name, city/state location, mobile number, email address and LinkedIn profile vanity URL.

Use your mobile number instead of a landline in the Contact Information Section of your resume.

So much of the hiring process these days can be done over text messaging. In fact, if a company is using an applicant tracking system they could very well be corresponding with you via text message as well as email. It's easy, convenient, and typically much more effective for getting a candidate's attention. That's why it's important to make sure you have a mobile phone number on your resume. This way you're not leaving out any modality that can be used to contact you.

Do not include your physical address for your main foundational public resume. You may need to add your physical address for specific online job applications to meet the requirements of submission, but for a general public document, don't include a physical address for security purposes.

**Is Your Resume Ready for Mobile Recruiting?**

Can your resume readily be viewed on a smartphone?

Your resume and job search have to now contend with smartphones, iPads, iPhones, Android phones and every other type of old and new tech device in between. The job search and the recruitment model is going mobile like the rest of business and every other industry—if they are smart and want to stay ahead of the competition.

So how can job seekers be ready for these technological adjustments and what should they expect?

- Make your communications ridiculously concise. Cover letters should be as short as a screenshot.
- Once your documents are done, plan to test your resume and cover letters on various mediums and devices to ensure they open and appear properly. I have been opening resumes on mobile devices since 2005. Some recruiters have been doing it much longer than I have. Resumes in dated Word versions have a lesser chance of opening on a newer phone. Are your Mac docs compatible with PC, Android, and other non-Mac gadgets? Can your PC-based docs open on iPhones and iPads? Plan to perform some quality controls with your documents and see what can open where.
- Use your mobile phone number on your resume—remove landlines from your applications. This will enable you to receive recruiting SMS text messages from employers who use this technology. ATS

(Applicant Tracking Systems) house this information in applicant data files and can send out mass job alerts via SMS text, as well as email, automated phone messages, etc. Landlines cannot receive texts—and who knows if your kids or elderly parents will answer the phone! Yikes!

**Graphs, Text Boxes & Tables**

While not always necessary, graphs, text boxes, and tables are a means to present your achievements quickly and effectively to a prospective employer. I suggest using documents with these elements for person-to-person networking via email and social communication platforms (such as Slack or LinkedIn).

Remember that your resume has only seconds to make an impression and stand out.

While I don't advocate these design elements for every resume, they can be very effective depending on your role or industry when used in a person-to-person context.

Applicant Tracking Systems (ATS), the software that is behind all of your online applications, has come a long way, but it still does not work well with complex graphic components. Items such as tables or special character bullets or shapes, do not come through well when you apply online. Use MS Word borders and shading functions to create simple, digestible graphic elements that will work in most of today's applicant systems.

In order to get around this, you can use a PDF version of your resume – but know that you may lose the keyword optimization strengths going this route. Another option is to have a simple version to use specifically for applying online. You can create a graphic-free version of your resume by removing the non-text elements and saving it as a .txt file. This file is as bare as you can get – and it will show you if any additional items need to be removed.

Similarly, when you apply to a position via email, you should minimize the graphic elements. You never know how the recruiter or hiring manager will be opening/viewing your resume, so it's best to be on the safe side to ensure a visually appealing resume – instead of a garbled mess.

**Nationwide Satellite TV | Princeton, NJ**  2017 - present
Satellite television service provider to US homes and businesses with 15,000 employees, 21 Million subscribers and $17.2 Billion in revenues.

**MANAGER, DIGITAL MARKETING**

*Recruited to devise and integrate marketing metrics for internal and external partners and to lead a 4-person team. In five months, increased click-through rates (CTR) by 16% and impressions by 22% for Q1-2020 vs. Q1-2019 for this $226 Million sales division.*

- Partnered with seven product groups to design and execute targeted email campaigns sent to 8 Million subscribers. Achieved a **12% sales increase on $226 Million** and **reached a market share goal of 23%**, up from 21.9%.
- Coordinated with the outside creative agency to **produce 60-80 email campaigns per month** using a segmented strategy integrated with social media. Generated 100 Million emails to customers per month.
- **Design creative briefs for 14% less cost** with internal product group, while generating 16% CTR increase for campaigns.

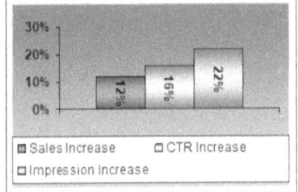

9
___

# THE EASY WAY TO FORMAT YOUR RESUME FOR ATS

Designing a resume that makes it through an applicant tracking system (ATS) to be read by a recruiter or hiring manager is the goal of every job seeker. Mastering how to format your executive resume for the ATS doesn't have to be hard. Following these simple steps to create an ATS complaint resume will improve your chances to landing that coveted interview. The over arching guideline is that when it comes to your online resume, simplicity is best.

**What is an Applicant Tracking System (ATS)?**

An applicant tracking system (ATS) is software that works like a resume database to help companies streamline their hiring process and review applications more quickly.

With paper applications being obsolete in a pandemic world combined with the volume of applicants increasing due to the economic crisis, the majority of companies have moved toward digital systems to track applicants while making sure their recruitment process complies with labor laws. Not only do these systems organize and sort applications, they also be screen candidates based on keyword content you include in your resume.

Common applicant tracking systems include, but are not limited to, Oracle Taleo, iCIMS, Bullhorn and Ascendify which all digest uploaded resumes submitted via job postings and emailed submissions.

**How does an ATS work?**

At a basic level, an ATS consists of opening new positions and posting them online via the company's corporate homepage or job boards. Once the position is open, all submitted applications are stored in a database. At this point, recruiters can search submissions using keywords and phrases to identify candidates to advance through the hiring process.

Many ATSs score applications and resumes based on parameters of the open position. Applicants are then ranked and sorted based on their score. You can think of it as the ATS doing the first screening instead of the recruiter.

It is important to note that not all ATSs are alike. Some systems can handle small graphics, while others can't. Some prefer pdfs while others require Word files. It's no surprise that your resume is at risk of getting lost in the shuffle with the varied document platforms.

While no process is foolproof, use this guide to better prepare your resume for an online application. See here for an example of an ATS-optimized resume.

**Step 1: Answer filter questions completely and properly**

A staggering 75% of resumes are never seen by employers, according to a 2019 CNBC article titled "75% of resumes are never read by a human—here's how to make sure your resume beats the bots", so it is important to start the process right. An

ATS typically screens candidates based on information provided in the application such as location and level of experience. Make sure to answer all the questions on the application, because when a question is left blank, the ATS may discard your resume. Completing all the information asked in an online application will improve your chances of your resume being seen by a person.

**Step 2: Format your resume in an ATS-friendly manner**

When applying online, avoid anything on your resume that could potentially clog the system. The key is to avoid templates and keep formatting simple.

- Title your resume with your name and targeted title—something like "Your Name – Marketing Director."
- Remove unique headings and stick to common resume headings like Work Experience, Education and Skills.
- Remove images, columns, tables, fields, text boxes and graphics so the ATS can quickly scan your text for keywords and phrases. The ATS may not be able to read data placed in images, tables, and text boxes, so it's best to avoid them altogether.
- Remove special characters and avoid creative or fancy bullets that are often illegible to an ATS scanner.
- Avoid special fonts, font treatments and colors. Stick to fonts such as Arial, Calibri, Cambria, Georgia, Impact, Courier, Lucinda, Tahoma or Trebuchet, and only use black color. Avoid underlining words, which can mess up the legibility of lower case letters such a g, j or y.
- Avoid spelling errors, since an ATS doesn't know

what you meant to write if you spell a keyword incorrectly.
- Include contact information in the body of your resume, not in the header or footer.
- Save your resume as a basic MS Word document (.docx), .pdf, .rtf or .txt file based on what is being asked for by the job posting.
- Avoid complex templates that are a combination of fixed fields and tables. These can confuse ATS systems. Also, avoid page numbers.
- When writing your employment history, present the information for each employer in the same order, i.e., company name, title, city, state, and date, and in reverse chronological order.

**Step 3: Focus on your resume's content**

Now that you've got the formatting nailed down, let's take a look at the actual content of the resume and make sure it is compatible with an ATS.

Beef up your skills section: To improve your chances of being discovered by the ATS, make sure to include any certifications you've received and mention any industry-specific terminology (ie. Salesforce for sales professionals or Oncology for healthcare professionals). Include both the spelled-out version and abbreviations of the same word.

Customize your resume: Optimize your professional summary with bulleted achievements and skills that relate to the job description. Then, find a natural way to include those keywords and phrases in your summary and throughout your resume.

You can also optimize your headers and titles based on the job description. Let's say you see the term "communication skills" sprinkled throughout the job description. In your resume, make sure you mention you "communication skills" as an exact phrase.

Don't overuse keywords: Do you need keywords? Absolutely. But stuffy keywords throughout your resume won't get you anywhere.

At the end of the day, make sure your ATS-optimized resume is simple, straightforward, and will delight both a machine and human reader. And by all means, feel free to use a more designed version of your resume to present once you land the job interview!

# 10

# HOW TO CHOOSE THE RIGHT RESUME WRITING PROFESSIONAL FOR YOU

If you need more support from a team of dedicated resume writing professionals, make sure you choose the right partner to help you get to where you want to be.

Identifying the best executive resume writer to design your resume and job search strategy can be a challenging task. How can you decide who is the best writer for your career goals? What criteria should you use in evaluating the writer's talents, credentials and capabilities?

When researching and selecting the best professional resume writer for you, I suggest that you find an employment and job search expert with both practical recruiting experience and executive resume writing expertise. The real world hiring experience of the resume writer can contribute heavily to the job seeker's success.

Use the following criteria when hiring an executive resume writer:

- Do they have search firm and/or corporate recruiting experience in their past career? What real world hiring and recruiting expertise do they have? How recent is that expertise?

- Have they worked directly with ATS systems before? Do they understand how resumes look in applicant tracking systems? Do they know how to format your resume accordingly?
- Do they provide resume samples of their work for you to review?
- How familiar are they with your industry?
- Do they know and teach effective job search tactics and understand the resume's role in that process to ensure the document is optimized and designed effectively?
- Do their resumes and job search techniques demonstrate articulated results?
- How many professional resume, job search, and career certifications do they have? Do they belong to career and HR-related organizations?
- What is their resume development and coaching process? Do you work with the writer one-on-one to help you invest in your resume package? Does the writer do all the work themselves or collaborate with a team behind them—and if so, do you still have the writer as your point person? Does the person who sold you the package partner you up with another writer on their team from the start? Are you filling out questionnaires only? Do you get to speak to the writer throughout the process?
- How familiar is your writer with social media and how good are their marketing skills? How prominent is their social media presence? Can you find them easily in many corners of the internet? (LinkedIn, Google Search, Facebook, Twitter, etc...)
- Is their business model a high-volume operation (low-cost subsidized by high volume of clients) or a low-volume operation (higher cost with a lower

volume of clients)? Do you need personalized attention? Higher priced resume writers will be able to spend more time with you on custom materials, whereas the lower priced resume writer will pull your information into a template so they can accommodate many clients fast.
- Do they charge for a detailed evaluation or offer free evaluations that cite common resume ailments? A detailed evaluation takes time and a busy writer, one who is in-demand, will charge for that detailed evaluation and give you actionable items to fix.
- What services are included and what additional services do they offer to ensure you can use the resume properly to land a job?
- Do they offer a satisfaction guarantee supporting all the work you'll do? Executive resume writers will not make promises they cannot keep or guarantee what they cannot control (i.e. market conditions and job seeker efforts). If they are genuinely interested in your success, they will not sign you on as a client if they believe they cannot help you to generate results.

If you'd like to find out more about how we work with clients, read on...

# NEXT STEPS

Now you've read through *The 6-Figure Resume*, you might be wondering what's next...

**For Dedicated DIY-ers**

If you're a dedicated DIY-er, you might want a little extra guidance in the form of a free webinar.

As a skilled professional struggling to land an interview, can you place yourself in one (or more) of the following categories?

- Colleagues telling you that your resume does not reflect how good you really are.
- Unhappy in your current job and eager to land the right job faster.
- Facing a career transition and need to showcase your experience to appeal to a new industry.

You're not the only one! Thousands of people, every day, are looking for employment under these same circumstances.

Your resume, along with most of theirs, is simply being passed over.

Why? Because it's boring and doesn't properly highlight your achievements. It's outdated. It leaves the reader confused about the position for which you are submitting. It doesn't tell them what they really want to know. And it doesn't make you sound like the expert you are.

Let's fix that.

During my free masterclass training, I'll share concrete, constructive, actionable feedback on how to fix common resume mistakes:

- What words to use to present yourself effectively, since what you're currently using hasn't worked well.
- How to structure your resume, taking into account what kind of information recruiters want to find, and where.
- How to make your resume achievement-driven, which delivers the results you offer straight into the recruiter's hands.

Bottom line: I understand how recruiters and hiring managers read resumes and how they choose candidates to interview based on those resumes. If you want to land interviews, you need to know how resumes work effectively in the job search process.

This free webinar is called *How to Design a Powerful Resume to Land Interviews and Get the Offer!* You can access it at www.chameleonresumes.com/awexecresreg

**Free Downloads**

It's much easier to put what you've learned into practice when you can see examples. So you can download a selection of resume samples and the 10-Minute Resume Cheat Sheet on our website.

- Resume samples at https://chameleonresumes.com/executive-resume-samples
- The 10-Minute Resume Cheat Sheet: https://resumecheatsheet.com/

**Dedicated Resume Writing Support**

If you'd like to find out more about working with us, our proven 4-stage META Job Landing System™ may be just what you're looking for.

It draws from our experience as corporate recruiters, executive search firm recruiters, and Fortune 500 HR consultants, and organizes your executive job search into focused stages.

Master the techniques behind presenting powerful documents, conducting impactful outreach, delivering unforgettable interviews, and confidently negotiating an incredible offer.

To schedule an exploratory call, visit our website: www.chameleonresumes.com/contact-us

# APPENDIX A
## THE CHAMELEON GUIDE TO ACTION VERBS

Use action verbs to tell your story with impact. They let you create impactful bullets that communicate clearly to hiring managers and resume readers exactly what you did and how you did it.

Pulled from the resumes created by Chameleon Resumes for our clients, the list below will enable you to create your own successful resume.

Remember: use present tense verbs with current positions and past tense verbs for previous roles.

- Grew
- Doubled
- Returned
- Constructed
- Spearheaded
- Led
- Integrated
- Reduced
- Served
- Evaluated
- Assessed

- Directed
- Managed
- Selected
- Compiled
- Presented
- Built
- Ensured
- Created
- Deployed
- Honored
- Named
- Marketed
- Sold
- Positioned
- Branded
- Communicated
- Drafted
- Consolidated
- Cultivated
- Volunteered
- Tested
- Contributed
- Collaborated
- Partnered
- Initiated
- Implemented
- Devised
- Designed
- Forecasted
- Tracked
- Hired
- Screened
- Supervised
- Inspected
- Strategized

- Supported
- Approved
- Organized
- Procured
- Researched
- Standardized
- Sourced
- Represented
- Processed
- Coordinated
- Orchestrated
- Oversaw
- Advise
- Played
- Interfaced
- Added
- Generated
- Produced
- Founded
- Received
- Restructured
- Structured
- Rebuilt
- Liaised
- Coached
- Consulted
- Executed
- Centralized
- Transitioned
- Moved
- Participated
- Discovered
- Introduced
- Investigated
- Conducted

- Assembled
- Authored
- Wrote
- Reported
- Facilitated
- Mediated
- Monitored
- Presided
- Qualified
- Moderated
- Promoted
- Performed
- Gathered
- Expanded
- Invited
- Arranged
- Crafted
- Prepared
- Recruited
- Prepared
- Testified
- Optimized
- Maximized
- Minimized
- Opened
- Helped
- Recalibrated
- Pitched
- Presented
- Achieved
- Accomplished
- Increased
- Decreased
- Established
- Shifted

# Appendix A

- Fostered
- Maintained
- Forged
- Chosen
- Repositioned
- Conceptualized
- Formulated
- Utilized
- Engineered
- Conceived
- Streamlined
- Counseled
- Outperformed
- Planned
- Administered
- Saved
- Exceeded
- Launched
- Negotiated
- Focused
- Cited
- Briefed
- Appointed
- Manifested

# APPENDIX B
## THE ULTIMATE RESUME CHECKLIST

Whether you currently have a resume or are creating one from scratch, this 35-point assessment checklist will help you get your resume in top-notch shape.

chameleonresumes.com  (917) 447-1815

## HOW DOES YOUR RESUME MEASURE UP?
## A 35-POINT ASSESSMENT CHECKLIST

Whether you currently have a resume or are creating one from scratch, this 35-Point Assessment Checklist will help you get your resume in top-notch shape. Use this list in conjunction with the Interview-Generating Resume Samples on page 19 to create an Interview-Generating Resume that will get the attention of employers.

### GETTING STARTED

1. ____Choose a contemporary font like Calibri or Arial Narrow for creative professions and a traditional font like Cambria or Garamond for conservative positions. Do not use ornate or script fonts. Fonts that vary too much from the accepted norms can leave negative impressions and will not be properly read by resume databases.

2. ____Use a type size between 10 and 12 for resume text. For section headings, use up to a 16-point size. Use 9 or 9.5 point type size for firm descriptions. Never use a type size smaller than 9 or larger than 16 for any reason.

3. ____Utilize a layout and design that reflect the position and compensation you are seeking. This is your marketing document. The font, borders, and layout choices of your resume should properly organize and clearly present your information to convey the appropriate image.

### CONTACT INFORMATION

4. ____Place your contact information at the top of the resume but not in the header. Resume databases and email previewers typically do not pick up information in headers or footers. Include your physical address, personal email address and cell phone number.

5. ____Include your social media links with your contact information. Include a personalized version of your LinkedIn Profile URL link, Facebook page and/or Twitter account under your name, address, phone number(s) and email address. Make sure that the links support your professional purpose and are not personal.

6. ____If you went to a top school and/or a school with a robust alumni network, use your school's email address (yourname@schoolname.edu). It's the best tool for objective branding without appearing like a braggart. Otherwise, make sure that your email address is neutral and professional, such as a Gmail email address.

7. ____Remove any section titled "Objective" that states what you are looking for in your next role or company. Employers want to learn what value and skills you will bring to their organization—not what you are looking for in your next role.

8. ____Create a branded title or heading for yourself that relates to job you are applying for. Here are some examples: Project Manager; Business Analyst; Versatile Office Manager; Marketing Communications Specialist. Make it easy for the reader to position you in the context of their company. This will also help communicate the job for which you are applying, even if your resume is separated from your cover letter. See The Branded Summary Section on page 16 and the Branded Resume Examples on page 19 to see how this can be done.

Copyright Chameleon Resumes © 2021

*Appendix B*

chameleonresumes.com  (917) 447-1815

9. \_\_\_\_Under your branded heading, create a bulleted key word section using phrases, topics and skills that you derive from job ads for the position you are targeting. Resume databases and recruiters use key phrases to source candidates; this list will help them find you and will make sure you are offering them exactly what they are asking for. See the Branded Resume Examples on page 19 to see how this can be done.

10. \_\_\_\_Use action verbs and nouns when writing your title and keyword section like 'profitable' and 'optimized.' Avoid subjective descriptions, such as reliable, excellent, best and cooperative.

## EMPLOYMENT SECTION

11. \_\_\_\_Save space on the first page by not using the heading 'Experience.' This will be obvious to the reader. However later in your resume, do use headings such as Skills, Interests, Education, Licenses, Certifications, Training/Professional Development, or Volunteer, as they make that information clear to the reader.

12. \_\_\_\_All employment bullets need to start with an action-driven verb. Use the **Action Verb Listing** on Page 11 to help you create strong employment bullets. Do not list job description responsibilities or a list of tasks. Do not use nouns to begin your bullets. Do not start with phrases like, "Duties included…" or "Responsible for", as this does not conjure an image of action, but a passive list of boring tasks.

13. \_\_\_\_Use present tense verbs for current positions currently held and past tense verbs for all past positions. Do not use first person pronouns anywhere in the resume…ever.

14. \_\_\_\_Do your bullets demonstrate how you can solve problems experienced by the prospective company? Ask this question for each bullet that you have listed on your resume. Review ads that describe the job you are seeking to ensure you are customizing your resume appropriately.

15. \_\_\_\_Include employment experience within the last 15-20 years. Do not cite jobs from more than 15-20 years ago. Exceptions to this rule can be jobs that resulted in earning a professional certification (i.e. CPA), or jobs with a top-tier company that demonstrate exceptional caliber and depth of experience (i.e. early Microsoft or Fortune 100 experience). Other than these exceptions, it is better to leave off experience from more than 2 decades ago.

16. \_\_\_\_Ensure your employment bullets cite measurable achievements. Show the results of your work using quantifiable references. Answer the question, "How do I know I did a good job?" with numbers for each bullet. Outline how you reduced expenses, increased revenue, optimized services or streamlined a process.
    EXAMPLE:
    o "Drove membership to highest level in organization's history" does not give a sense of from how many to how many. If you write "Drove membership from 50 to 75" or "Drove membership from 1500 to 4500", those are two different experiences, despite both starting the sentence with "Drove membership…" The numbers give context to your achievements.

chameleonresumes.com  (917) 447-1815

17. \_\_\_Give a sense of size and scope of your previous and/or current employer.
    EXAMPLE:
    o If you list, 'Managed financials for this start-up division of this progressive Fortune 500 firm', there is no sense of the size of the budget. It is better to write the bullet as, 'Managed the $400,000 budget for this start-up division of this progressive Fortune 500 firm.' This gives a greater sense of the size and scope of the environment where you worked.

18. \_\_\_Structure your promotions at one company under a single company heading. Do not show them as jobs under separate company headings. Using separate headings gives the impression that you had roles at different companies, when in actuality, you were promoted. Listing your progress under one heading demonstrates that you had career progression at one company versus different companies. See page 19 for an example with the Branded Resume Samples.

19. \_\_\_Accentuate the positive attributes in your background and de-emphasize the negative with placement, font treatment (bold, italics, and underlining).
    EXAMPLE:
    o If you worked for great companies, make the company names more prominent by listing them first. If you have relevant job titles but you are looking to switch industries, downplay the company names where you worked and emphasize the titles you held.

## EDUCATION SECTION

20. \_\_\_Schooling should be at the bottom of your resume unless (a) you graduated within the last year or (b) you graduated within 2-3 years from an area of study that is related to the work you are pursuing and it is a different field from your past/current work experience.

21. \_\_\_Include your GPA if you graduated within the past 5 years and your GPA was above a 3.0.

22. \_\_\_If you graduated from school over 15 years ago, you do not need to include the year of graduation. Always include honors and honor societies from universities/colleges.

23. \_\_\_Unless you are a recent college graduate, you do not need to include job experiences or activities performed while in school.

24. \_\_\_Once you have obtained your Bachelor's degree, don't list your Associate's degree.

## Appendix B

chameleonresumes.com          (917) 447-1815

### ADDITIONAL SECTIONS

25. ___When listing volunteer / professional affiliations, utilize the same parameters as listing an employer. Give yourself an appropriate title like 'Membership Coordinator' or 'Financial Manager' instead of 'Volunteer.' If you have this experience listed in a section entitled Volunteer, it is understood you are/were a volunteer. Craft achievement-driven bullets outlining goals met in fundraising, membership increases, budgets managed, programs administered, groups coordinated and other crucial functions that had impact.

26. ___Remove any clubs/associations that relate to religious, political or controversial issues.

27. ___Ensure that any software skills you list are current and relevant to today's marketplace.

28. ___If you have them, list language skills other than English on your resume. If you are bi-lingual, do not list English as one of your languages for domestic positions. It is implied. If the bi-lingual skills are highly pertinent to the position being applied to, consider including this in the branded summary at the top of the resume.

29. ___Do not add any references to your resume and remove the 'References Available Upon Request' statement at the bottom of your resume. It is understood that references will be provided if asked during the interview process—so do not waste the space stating the obvious.

### OVERALL ANALYSIS & REVIEW

30. ___If you have a 2+ page resume, ask yourself, 'Am I keeping the reader interested in 5-10 second increments to ensure they read the subsequent pages?" Just because you have a two- or three- page resume does not mean it will be read.

31. ___Do not insert graphics, text boxes or tables into your resume. These are not digested by resume databases very well. Use the borders/shading function in MS Word to simple create design elements without inserting lines or complex graphical components.

32. ___Test your resume online and on paper. Print it out and see that it lays out the way you expected. Open up the document to view it on your computer screen—does it format as you expected? Make sure there are no odd page breaks.

33. ___Put your name, contact information (email/phone number only) and page number on subsequent pages and addendums of your resume.

34. ___Can your resume be read on most commonly used PDA devices and within resume databases? This is worth exploring since most people do not work in front of a PC all day anymore. To create a text-only resume (called an ASCII Resume) for entering into online job applications that populate resume databases, save your resume as a .txt file.

35. ___Put your bullets to the test:
    o Are they easy to understand?
    o Could you say the bullet phase aloud and it makes sense?
    o Would it make sense to someone not in the industry?

Copyright Chameleon Resumes © 2021

Now you've finished auditing your resume, you can take the next step to rebuild the sections of your resume that need more work—or start over. This will ensure you have the best branded resume to showcase your skills effectively.

Use this list in conjunction with the Interview-Generating Resume Samples to create an Interview-Generating Resume that will get the attention of employers.

You can download the samples from here: https://chameleonresumes.com/executive-resume-samples

Do you have further questions? Please visit www.chameleonresumes.com

# ABOUT THE AUTHOR

Lisa Rangel is the founder and managing director of Chameleon Resumes, named a *Forbes* Top 100 Career Website.

At Chameleon Resumes, she has assembled the best team of executive resume writers and job landing consultants who all have prior search firm and corporate recruiting experience. Lisa and her team know first-hand which resumes land interviews, as they have worked successfully with clients in 84 countries. She was hired as a moderator of LinkedIn premium career groups and career blogger for eight years.

As a recruitment professional for 13 years prior to opening Chameleon in 2009, Lisa has developed a career document writing and job landing process that draws from first hand-recruitment experience to accelerate the job landing process for her clients. She has held management and producer roles in numerous companies, ranging from international recruitment conglomerates to focused executive search firms after graduating from Cornell University..

Lisa is a member of the National Resume Writers' Association and Professional Association of Resume Writers and Career Coaches.

She has been featured in person, online and in print on Fast Company, Forbes, LinkedIn, Newsweek, Money, Business Insider, CNBC, BBC, Crain's New York, Chicago Tribune, CIO Magazine, American Marketing Association, eFinancial Careers, The Vault, Monster, U.S. News & World Report,

Good Morning America, Fox Business News and many other reputable publications.

She is the author of nine books, creator of the Get Hired Fast job-landing training series, and a serial advice giver through her website ChameleonResumes.com. You can sign up to get advice from Lisa directly into your inbox from chameleonresumes.com/get-daily-career-tips/.

**in** linkedin.com/in/lisarangel

# ALSO BY LISA RANGEL

The Job Landing Mindset

www.ingramcontent.com/pod-product-compliance
Lightning Source LLC
Chambersburg PA
CBHW032047290426
44110CB00012B/989